New Zealand
A Visual Souvenir

Gareth Eyres

First published in 1999 by New Holland Kowhai
an imprint of New Holland Publishers (NZ) Ltd
Auckland • Sydney • London • Cape Town

218 Lake Road Northcote Auckland New Zealand
14 Aquatic Drive Frenchs Forest NSW 2086 Australia
24 Nutford Place London W1H 6DQ United Kingdom
80 McKenzie Street Cape Town 8001 South Africa

Copyright © 1999 in photography: Gareth Eyres/Exposure
with the exception of the following images:
pages 18, 19, 53, 56, 57, 59 David Wall;
page 39 Rob Suisted; and page 17 Ian Baker

Copyright © 1999 in text: Susan Buckland
Copyright © 1999 New Holland Publishers (NZ) Ltd

ISBN: 1 877246 17 4

Managing Editor: Renée Lang

Design: Sally Hollis-McLeod/Moscow Design

Colour reproduction by Colour Symphony Pte Ltd
Printed by Craft Print Pte Ltd, Singapore

Front cover: The snowy slopes of Mt Tongariro, central North Island.
Back cover: Awaroa Bay, South Island.
Inside back flap: Pohutukawa, New Zealand's Christmas tree.
End pages: Abel Tasman National Park, South Island.
Title page: Mt Taranaki, North Island.
Right: Waikato dairy herds, North Island.

INTRODUCTION

From the boiling fury of the North Island thermal plateau to the soaring alps of the South Island, New Zealand is a land of great extremes. One of the last countries in the world to be colonised by humans because of its isolation in the temperate latitudes of the South Pacific, the land evolved through ice ages and glaciers and massive volcanic eruptions. Mountain ranges thrust skyward, seeds borne on the air and water took hold in the rich soil and birds thrived in thick forests free of ground predators.

This island nation, still young and evolving, and with remarkable scenic diversity in and around its long, narrow shape, attracts a huge number of visitors from far and wide.

Left: The tussock and hill surrounds of the South Island Mackenzie Country are etched on the waters of Lake Alexandrina.
Overleaf: The Cape Reinga lighthouse stands lonely vigil at the tip of the North Island. From its cliff top the lighthouse overlooks the Tasman Sea as it surges into the opposing force of the Pacific Ocean. According to Maori legend, the spirits of the dead depart for their ancestral homeland from this northern end of the country.

Previous pages: Some of New Zealand's earliest European migrants settled on the shores of the Hokianga Harbour in the far north of New Zealand. From the 1840s the ships came sailing past the massive sand dunes and up the wide stretches of water. The settlements were gradually overtaken by larger cities to the south and, today, people travel to the far north for the tranquillity and history of the Hokianga.

Left: The lush Waipoua Forest on the west coast of Northland is interrupted only by water. The state forest has some of the last great stands of kauri, New Zealand's magnificent hardwood that covered much of Northland before settlers discovered its quality and felled it for buildings and boat masts. Tane Mahuta, lord of the forest (right), is estimated to be 1200 years old.

Right: The Bay of Islands, the centre of New Zealand's early colonial history, has become an idyllic holiday location. Boating and game fishing are favourite pastimes among the 150 islands and extensive coastline.

Above: At Waitangi in the Bay of Islands, this Maori meeting house was built in 1940 to commemorate the signing of the Treaty of Waitangi a century earlier.

Previous pages: Like a slender rocket poised for take-off, Auckland's Sky Tower rises from the city above the harbour's shimmering waters, framed by the harbour bridge.

Left: At Kohimaramara Beach, only a few kilometres from downtown Auckland, young sailors test their skills with P Class yachts. Rangitoto Island is a brooding presence in the background.

Above: Less than an hour by ferry from Auckland City, Waiheke Island on the Hauraki Gulf has become popular as both a holiday retreat and an offshore suburb.

Hahei Beach (right) and Cathedral Cove (left) are typical of the golden sand beaches on the Coromandel, an eastern peninsula that extends into the Hauraki Gulf. The Coromandel also has a vigorous gold rush history.

Above: A traditional tribal carving receives strong competition at Rotorua, still a strong centre of Maoridom in New Zealand.

Right: A fisherman casts his rod as dawn rises on Lake Rotorua. The central plateau is a trout-fishing mecca with many other lakes – including Lake Taupo – within an hour's drive of Rotorua.

Previous pages: Sunlight plays on the ferns and river boulders of native forest in the central North Island.

Right: Pohutu, godfather of geysers at the Whakarewarewa thermal valley in Rotorua, vents his fury.

Above: On the outskirts of Rotorua, Waiotapu Valley turns on its thermal magic.

Left: From Lake Taupo the outflowing Waikato River hurtles down to the Huka Falls. The riverbed drops eight metres before plunging another 11 metres over the falls where the thundering waters attract thousands of sightseers.

Above: A jetboat skims over the Waikato River. From its source at Lake Taupo the Waikato, New Zealand's longest river, winds across to the western shores of the North Island.

Previous pages: The cone of Mt Ngauruhoe wears a winter mantle of snow. Rising from the central plateau Ngauruhoe and her mighty neighbour, Mt Ruapehu, are still active volcanoes. With Mt Tongariro, they form a majestic trio at the southern end of Lake Taupo.

Above: The moon rises over Mt Ngauruhoe and bathes it in a soft magenta light.

Right: The winter snows on the slopes of Mt Ngauruhoe are no deterrent to hikers, keen to breathe the mountain air and drink in the stunning views of the surrounding volcanic plateau and lakes.

As they have done for generations, thousands of gannets nest from November to February on the rocky plateau at Cape Kidnappers in Hawke's Bay. From the gannet colony on the tip of Cape Kidnappers, Hawke's Bay curves in a wide crescent around to the northeast towards Gisborne, the first city in the world to greet the sun each day.

Overleaf: Protected by a backbone of ranges from the prevailing westerly wind, vineyards flourish in the sunny Hawke's Bay climate. The long-established farming region now produces some of New Zealand's best wines.

Wellington, New Zealand's capital city, concertinas from a shawl of hills and spreads in a dress circle around the harbour.

Left: The Marlborough Sounds at the northeastern tip of the South Island shelter hundreds of placid coves and bush-clad inlets. Many can only be reached by boat, which adds to their charm.

Above: Ferries carrying passengers between the North and South Island ports of Wellington and Picton pass each other in the Tory Channel. The inter-island ferries also shuttle cars and railway wagons across Cook Strait several times a day.

Left: Hikers pause to admire views of Abel Tasman National Park.
The South Island park contains one of the country's most scenic walks, incorporating both coast and bush.

Above: Close encounters with seals are among the pleasures of kayaking in the sea off Abel Tasman National Park. The area is also renowned for its golden sand beaches and clear waters.

Overleaf: In the wild expanse of Awaroa Bay in Abel Tasman Park thick native forest coats the hills and runs almost to the water's edge.

Left: This sightseeing helicopter looks like a small dragonfly as it flies over the massive ice block formations of Fox Glacier on the West Coast of the South Island.

Above: An exhilarating South Island adventure is to land by helicopter on the glacier and crunch over its icy path.

Overleaf: The Tasman Sea folds into lonely Gillespies Beach below Fox Glacier. Cut off from the east coast by the Southern Alps, the ruggedly beautiful west side of the South Island is sparsely populated.

Left: North of Christchurch on the east coast, the rocky foreshore of Kaikoura drifts across to the mountain ranges of the same name.

Above: Schools of whales frequent the waters off the coast and whale watching has become a popular activity in the area.

Left: Oblivious to the dramatic mountain backdrop, sheep graze on the green pastures of a Kaikoura farm.

Above: A cattle farm sits snugly in the foothills of the Kaikoura ranges. Despite the loss of Britain as a major market for New Zealand's agricultural products, the wool, meat and dairy industries have remained primary exports for the country.

Left: Students from Christchurch Boys High School enjoy a late summer game of rugby, New Zealand's favourite sport game.

Below: Trams have disappeared from other main New Zealand cities, but not from Christchurch. Here passengers disembark in colourful New Regent Street.

Right: Dwarfed by its grand surroundings, the solitary Church of the Good Shepherd sits on the shores of Lake Tekapo. It was built in 1935 as a memorial to the pioneer sheep farmers of the South Island highlands.

Above: The magnificent crown of Mt Cook stabs the sky. Maori call this great mountain Aoraki, 'cloud in the sky'. Standing 3764 metres high, it is New Zealand's highest mountain and undisputed king of the Southern Alps.

Above: Lanarch Castle is an interesting amalgam of Dunedin's Victorian and Scottish architecture. Member of parliament and banker William Lanarch built it in the 1870s and no expense was spared in the construction. Today it is a popular tourist attraction.

Right: Otago University is another example of Dunedin's fine colonial architecture. The university's vibrant campus attracts many students from the length and breadth of New Zealand and beyond.

Right: The hilly Otago Peninsula traces Otago Harbour out to Taiaroa Head, perhaps the only reserve in the world where one can drive up to see a colony of Royal albatross. Access is controlled, but the remarkable birds with their huge wingspans are clearly visible.

Above: The shy hoiho, or yellow-eyed penguin, is a protected species in New Zealand. These rare penguins – unique to New Zealand – can be seen out on the tip at Taiaroa Head, waddling in and out of the ocean.

Left: The stark St Bathans cliffs drop sheer into the lake in South Otago. From the 1860s through to the early 20th century, the outskirts of the township of St Bathans was the site of much gold mining activity.

Above: The Vulcan Hotel in the township of St Bathans has changed little since it was built in 1869.

Overleaf: Like velvet veils, the Purakaunui Falls cascade over rocky steps through the bush in the Catlins, a dramatic slice of the southeast coast of the South Island. Ancient virgin forests, sandy beaches where few people go, and mysterious 30-metre high cathedral caves are features of the region.

Left: From the top of the Remarkables mountain range are sweeping views of Lake Wakatipu and the alpine town of Queenstown, cradled by an ampitheatre of mountains.

Above: Bungy jumping is an adrenalin-pumping experience that many cannot resist.

Above: Autumn burnishes the forests of Arrowtown, 20 kilometres from Queenstown.

Right: The site of rich gold diggings last century, Skippers Canyon is reached by a narrow, snaking road high above precipitous cliffs. The road follows a bridle path hewn from the rocks in the 1880s – the rewards are splendidly rugged views and fascinating history.

Above: The rapids of the Landsborough River near Queenstown provide plenty of excitement for white water rafters. Trips can last from two hours to several days and safety regulations are stringent.

Right: Queenstown's fast-flowing rivers and narrow gorges provide exciting jetboat rides. New Zealander Sir William Hamilton invented the powerful, shallow-draught jetboat. Skilled drivers race passengers in a thrilling ride across the Dart River current to within safe distances of the steep banks.

Left: Over the hill from Queenstown is the Treble Cone skifield at Wanaka. Views of valleys, lakes and mountains greet skiers as they whizz down the slopes.

Right: A skier becomes airborne over a slope at Treble Cone skifield. The skifields of the Southern Alps not only offer heart-thumping views, but a range of slopes varying from gentle to challenging.

The summer sun warms Lake Hayes near Queenstown, New Zealand's best-known all seasons resort. One of several exquisite lakes in the area, Lake Hayes attracts an increasing number of people during the Christmas holiday season.

Mountains and flax bushes fuse in the Mirror Lakes
of the Eglington Valley in Fiordland.

Bush clings to the mountain passes along Fiordland's
world-famous Milford Track. The 1.2 million-hectare
Fiordland National Park is a place of beautiful, deep
and lonely fiords, rain forest, waterfalls and some
of New Zealand's rarest native birds. The vast region
is protected and parts of it remain only partly explored
to this day.

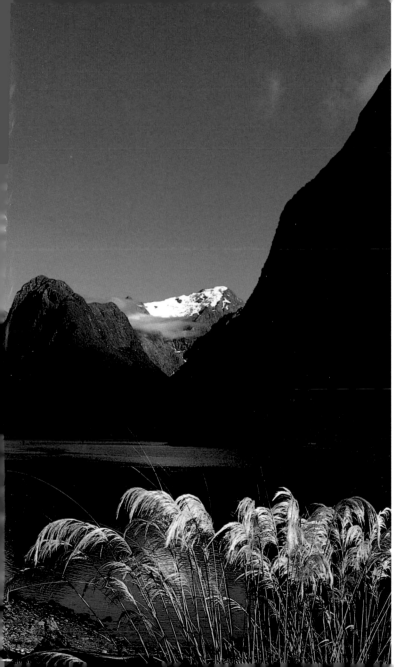

Mitre Peak thrusts 1695 metres up from Milford Sound towards the sky. People come from all around the globe to visit this World Heritage area.

Almost impenetrable native forest accompanies a launch cruising
up Dusky Sound, which was named by British explorer Captain
James Cook who entered the fiords on his second voyage of 1773.